Looking Inside a 3D Printer

By Quenton Oakes

CHERRY LAKE Publishing

Published in the United States of America by
Cherry Lake Publishing
Ann Arbor, Michigan
www.cherrylakepublishing.com

Series Adviser: Kristin Fontichiaro
Reading Adviser: Marla Conn, MS, Ed., Literacy specialist,
Read-Ability, Inc.
Photo Credits: Cover, Marla Keays / tinyurl.com/gkrn3g2 /
CC BY 2.0; pages 4 and 10, courtesy of Michigan Makers;
all other photos by Quenton Oakes

Library of Congress Cataloging-in-Publication Data
Names: Oakes, Quenton, author.
Title: Looking inside a 3D printer / by Quenton Oakes.
Other titles: 21st century skills innovation library. Makers as innovators.
Description: Ann Arbor, Michigan : Cherry Lake Publishing, [2017] | Series: Makers
as innovators junior | Series: 21st century skills innovation library | Audience: K to
grade 3. | Includes bibliographical references and index.
Identifiers: LCCN 2016032423| ISBN 9781634721899 (lib. bdg.) | ISBN
9781634723213 (pbk.) | ISBN 9781634722551 (pdf) | ISBN 9781634723879 (ebook)
Subjects: LCSH: Three-dimensional printing—Juvenile literature. | Computer printers—
Juvenile literature.
Classification: LCC TS171.95 .O25 2017 | DDC 621.9/88—dc23 LC record available at
https://lccn.loc.gov/2016032423

Cherry Lake Publishing would like to acknowledge the work of the Partnership for
21st Century Learning. Please visit *www.p21.org* for more information.

Printed in the United States of America
Corporate Graphics

A Note to Adults: Please review the instructions for the activities in this book before allowing children to do them. Be sure to help them with any activities you do not think they can safely complete on their own.

A Note to Kids: Be sure to ask an adult for help with these activities when you need it. Always put your safety first!

Table of Contents

3D printers are changing the way many things are made.

What Is a 3D Printer?

There are many different ways of making things. For example, you might paint a picture or sew a shirt. One new way to make things is 3D printing. With a 3D printer, you can create an object on a computer. Then your computer tells the 3D printer what to create. Soon, you will have a plastic version of your object. Then you see what it looks like in the real world!

Filament comes in many different colors and sizes.

Printing with Plastic

3D printers make things out of a special type of plastic. This plastic is called **filament**. 3D printers melt filament into liquid. Then they build things by drawing with the melted filament. When the melted filament cools, it turns solid again.

Where Can You Find a 3D Printer?

Some libraries and schools have 3D printers. Ask your teachers or parents if they can show you one. Maybe you can even print an object of your own!

3D printers help us print fun toys and even practical things like this nut and bolt.

Where Did 3D Printers Come From?

3D printers were first used in factories in the 1980s. These factories used the printers to quickly make **prototypes**. Factories often have to build many versions of a prototype. 3D printed prototypes can help designers check that prototype pieces will fit together perfectly.

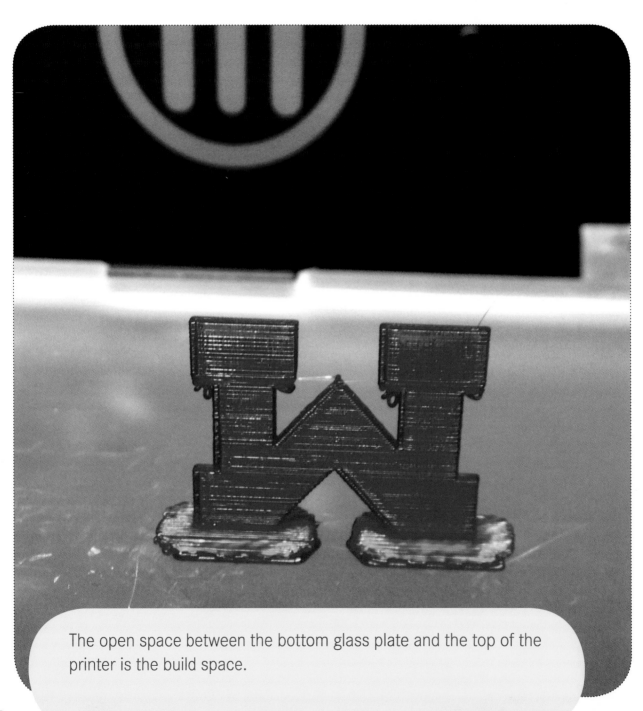

The open space between the bottom glass plate and the top of the printer is the build space.

Big and Small

A 3D printer can only make things that fit inside of its **build space**. Most 3D printers are small enough to fit on a desk. They can only print small objects. But others are big enough to take up a whole room. The biggest ones can print a whole house!

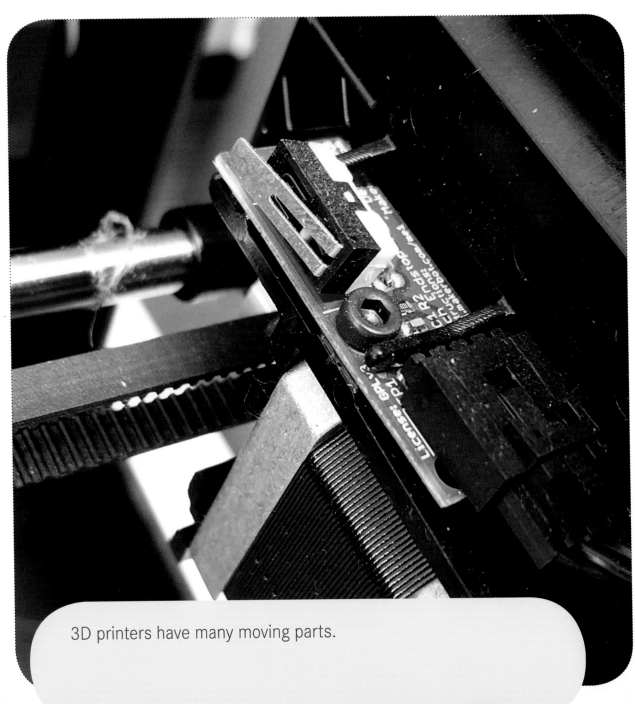

3D printers have many moving parts.

Layer by Layer

3D printers make things by drawing very thin layers of melted filament. They make taller shapes by stacking many layers on top of each other. 3D printers have to draw each layer one at a time. Some objects can be over 100 layers tall. Imagine having to draw 100 pictures just to make one thing!

Think Like a 3D Printer

Try drawing yourself like a 3D printer draws. Start with the bottoms of your feet. Then draw the tops of your feet. Then draw your legs. Keep going all the way to the top of your head. That's how 3D printers print out shapes.

3D printers come in many shapes and sizes. This printer can make items that are over 2 feet (61 centimeters) tall.

All Kinds of Printers

There are many different kinds of 3D printers. Some come from stores. Others are homemade. Some can do special things that others can't. For example, some can print things from metal, concrete, or even food! Even though these machines are all a little different, they are all still 3D printers.

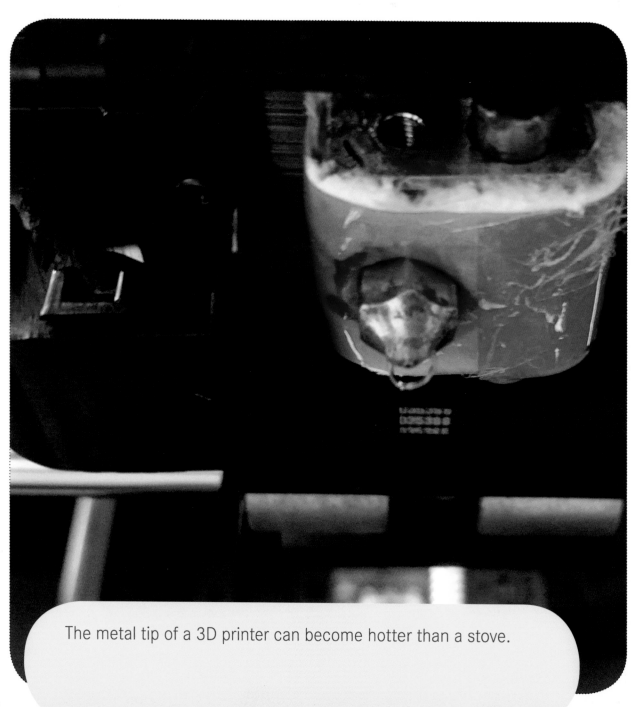

The metal tip of a 3D printer can become hotter than a stove.

Heating Up

The extruder head is the piece of a 3D printer that melts the filament. It moves around to draw an object. It always needs to be cleaned before printing. If it isn't clean, you will see it move around. But no melted filament will come out of it.

Safety First!

3D printers get very hot while they are working. Never try to touch a 3D printer unless you are sure it is cool. Ask an adult to help you with 3D printing projects.

Shapes printed from a 3D printer are mostly empty inside.

Filling in the Gaps

Watch a 3D printer while it's running. You will see inside your object as it prints. Your object will likely look solid on the outside. But it will probably be filled with little plastic shapes. This is called **infill**. Infill makes prints strong. This helps them hold their shape. Infill can be shaped like honeycombs, squares, or triangles. Infill also uses less filament. This helps save money.

After your print is done, you can clean it to make it look even better. This is a 3D print of a clip-on bow tie.

Finishing Touches

When the printer is done and has cooled off, ask an adult to help you remove the print. He or she may need a metal spatula to get it off. Objects often have extra pieces of plastic on them when they come out of the printer. You can use sandpaper to help smooth these out. You can also ask an adult to help you cut off the extra pieces. Once your object looks good, you're all done. What will you print next?

Glossary

build space (BILD SPAYS) the amount of space that a 3D printer can use to make things

filament (FIL-uh-mint) the thin strands of plastic that 3D printers use to make things

infill (IN-fil) plastic shapes inside a 3D-printed object that make it stronger

prototypes (PROH-toh-types) test versions of an invention or product

Find Out More

Books

O'Neill, Terence, and Josh Williams. *3D Printing*. Ann Arbor, MI: Cherry Lake Publishing, 2013.

Roslund, Samantha, and Emily Puckett Rodgers. *Makerspaces*. Ann Arbor, MI: Cherry Lake Publishing, 2014.

Zizka, Theo. *3D Modeling*. Ann Arbor, MI: Cherry Lake Publishing, 2015.

Web Sites

Cookie Caster
www.cookiecaster.com
Create your own cookie cutter that you can 3D print.

Thingiverse
www.thingiverse.com
Practice using your 3D printer by printing downloadable 3D models made by others from this site.

Tinkercad
www.tinkercad.com
Make your own 3D models for printing.

Index

About the Author

Quenton Oakes makes all kinds of things, especially ones that light up. He wants to be a librarian when he grows up.